T0196312

Miniatures of a Zen Master

Miniatures *of a*
Zen Master

Robert Aitken

Introduction by Nelson Foster

COUNTERPOINT · BERKELEY

The Library of Congress has catalogued the hardcover as follows:

Aitken, Robert.
Miniatures of a Zen master / Robert Aitken ;
with an introduction by Nelson Foster.
p. cm.
ISBN-13: 978-1-58243-441-4
ISBN-10: 1-58243-441-7
1. Religious life—Zen Buddhism. I. Title.
BQ9286.2.A37 2008
294.3′4432—dc22
2008013039

Paperback ISBN: 978-1-58243-536-7

Book design by Gopa & Ted2, Inc.
Printed in the United States of America

COUNTERPOINT
2560 Ninth Street, Suite 318
Berkeley, CA 94710
www.counterpointpress.com

for Gina

Table of Contents

Book II

Book III

Book IV

Introduction

THIS LITTLE BOOK contains the late thoughts of one of America's first native-born Zen masters, set down at the age of ninety by a man looking back on (and still putting to good use) the experiences of an extraordinary life. They read not as after-thoughts, intended to correct or improve earlier staements, so much aas manifestations of a fresh turn of mind that has come both unexpectedly and in due course. This is a late work, too, as a capping achievement in a long career of teaching and writing, thirteenth in the string of books that Robert Aitken has devoted, quite variously, to his one great topic and passion, Zen Buddhism. Not a few of its contents are late thoughts in a simple, nocturnal sense as well—inspirations that visited at night as Aitken Rōshi awaited or awoke from sleep. In the early stages of preparing the book, frustrated by the number of half-dreamt ideas that escaped by morning, he positioned a digital recorder by the bedside, with which to capture phrases for retrieval and evaluation in the light of day.

Readers familiar with Aitken Rōshi's previous writings may discover a resemblance between the short prose of this book and that of *Encouraging Words*, published in 1993. Like items in the "Words in the Dōjō" section of that earlier collection, a number of these "miniatures" originally were spoken into the stillness of the dōjō, or Zen training hall, to guide and spur on the group sitting in zazen. Other miniatures bear a marked similarity in spirit to the pithy essays he has produced for decades, in which a news item, a colorful turn of phrase, a line of literature, or a chance encounter becomes the point of departure for pungent instruction in the way of practice and realization. As before, Aitken Rōshi is urging us along the path of Zen, and his teaching crackles now with a zeal that surely results, at least in part, from the medical crises and physical diminutions he has weathered in recent years. More than ever, he speaks as an elder, with the power and poignancy of that vantage.

These pages are charged also with Rōshi's fervor for a profound change of course in society as a whole. Railing against prejudice, injustice, war, and the ravaging of cultures, places, and the many beings, finned or feathered, flowering or fungal, is no novelty for Aitken Rōshi, but he expresses his abhorrence here with a new-found freedom. World events have prompted this forthrightness, and again aging has played a part, I think: the beauty and preciousness of life, viewed from his pinnacle of years, has made callousness and cruelty yet more inexplicable and intolerable, and old inhibitions have dropped away besides.

Even more striking and delightful than the continuities between this book and Aitken Rōshi's past work are its differences, not just in tone but especially in subject matter. A decade of persistent, low-key campaigning utterly failed to persuade him to prepare, if not a full-scale autobiography, at least episodic memoirs—until this publication. We owe the opportunity to read the mainly fond, sometimes painful reminiscences herein to a twin development that has overridden his disinclination to write about himself. Early memories have assumed increasing prominence, as they so often do with the waning of short-term recall. Far more important, a new reason to record those memories arrived two years ago in the figure of his first, long-anticipated grandchild—Gina, whose name you may have noticed on the dedication page. What more vivid impetus could there be for a writer? We who enjoy these biographical tales ought to reckon ourselves beneficiaries of his blonde-headed charmer.

Our author being who he is, a man of letters from head to faraway toe, we also have his literary predecessors to thank for the wee treats that follow. Precedents count, both in Buddhism and in writing, and Aitken Rōshi has not been one to ignore them. His models in the genre of brief nonfiction, he says, start with Logan Pearsall Smith, whose *Trivia* fascinated him in college. More obviously, they include three writers he cites in the text: the haiku poet Bashō, who set the poems of his travel diaries in brilliant bits of prose; Thoreau, whose journals Aitken Rōshi has long relished; and the four-teenth-century Japanese Buddhist priest Yoshida Kenkō. Another certifiable influence is the Ming-dynasty Chinese layman Hong Zicheng, whose *Vegetable Roots Dis-*

course Aitken Rōshi translated and published in 2006, in collaboration with his old friend Daniel Kwok.

Both Hong and Kenkō practiced a style of writing known in Japan as *zuihitsu*, literally "following the brush." (Donald Richie has suggested the term "spontaneous nattering" for this venerable literary form, accurately conveying its air of informality. "Jottings," one might render the term, if nattering seems too undignified.) In a miniature titled "Bishop Ditch," Aitken Rōshi reprises a passage from Kenkō's *Tsurezuregusa* and explicitly claims that book as his precedent, which indeed seems apt. If he has let his electronic "brush" run more freely than ever in drafting these pages, a share of credit is due the retired courtier and priest of fourteenth-century Kyoto as well as the little girl capering at her grandpa's knee.

I am grateful beyond measure for the confluence of elements that has brought this book into existence, most crucially, of course, the remarkable longevity and vitality of my old teacher. I would be remiss if I neglected to express continuing thanks, on behalf of all who love Aitken Rōshi, to those he names in his acknowledgments. With publication of this book, we are indebted especially to the team of caregivers, both paid and volunteer, who have nursed him through thick and thin and to his loyal secretary, Carolyn Glass, whose attentions to the manuscript, not to mention its author, have often far exceeded the call of duty.

—Nelson Foster, Ring of Bone Zendo,
San Juan Ridge, California

Miniatures

Book I

Intimacy

INTIMACY IS THE quality of your practice and of your realization. It is the vast interior that knows no exterior. It is the great echo-chamber of your *Mu*,[1] of your breath counting—"one, two, three . . ." It is not coterminal with anything. Only you as a human being can know this marvelous place of practice.

The Virtue of Distraction

THINKING ABOUT YOURSELF and your doings marks your distraction. Thinking about these words is also distracting. That's okay. Let your distraction remind you. Whatever happens, it is the Bodhisattva[2] Kanzeon[3] taking you by the hand. Distraction is your good fortune, popping up for you to use.

Buddha's Birthday

IN THE ANNUAL ceremony of pouring sweet tea over an image of the baby Buddha, we are purifying our own baby Buddha. Our baby Buddha is our own innocent nature. It is the silence and total absence of thought about a separate *me*. Once a year on the Buddha's birthday we overtly share our promises to restore our own original innocence. Once a moment we share them by example.

The Tangled Web

WALTER SCOTT WROTE: "Oh, what a tangled web we weave, / When first we practice to deceive." You and I aren't practicing deception deliberately, but we are content to let our minds fall into a deceptive mode. That's the problem in a nutshell. It presents itself with every breath. We forget our role as the Bodhisattva Kanzeon. We allow our self-concerns to obscure the way. But really, "Mu" is simply "Mu"—nothing more.

Therapy

SOME PEOPLE THINK of Zen practice as a kind of therapy. That's not completely mistaken, of course. Yamada Kōun Rōshi[4] used to say that the practice of Zen is to forget the self in the act of uniting with something— Mu, or breath counting, or the song of a thrush. That is wonderful therapy. Concern about *me* and *mine* disappears.

Lucky

SOMETIMES WHEN I would complain unreasonably, my father would say, "You're lucky to be alive." I thought the old man was just rehashing his aphorisms. Now after studying a bit of biology, I see his point. You are indeed lucky to be alive. Moreover, you're incredibly fortunate to find yourself in a made-to-order dōjō[5] with a splendid teacher. Now the ball is in your court.

Vows

GREAT MASTERS of the past were once as confused as you and I. They tell how they renewed their vows: "Even if it takes me for the rest of my life, I will devote myself resolutely to making it possible for my latent Buddhas to do their work. Even if I'm not successful, I devote myself right here to the very end." Now it's our turn. Your turn. My turn.

The Timeless

You have plenty of time—that is to say, you face the timeless. It is there that the moment of realization occurs. However, any concept of the timeless or of realization is the realm of here-and-there. You are just sitting with your thoughts. Dismiss all concepts. Dismiss all thoughts. *Neti, neti, neti.* Not this, not this, not this.

Liking Yourself

A LOT OF US start out on the practice because we don't accept ourselves fully. Under good tutelage we find ourselves in a process of forgetting ourselves, and realize that this is really the way to uncover the unique one that has been there all along. Give the Tao a chance. Give yourself a chance.

Doubt

EFFORT ALONE will get you nowhere, except maybe to the Slough of Despond. Your work must be doubt, that is, it must be your all-consuming spirit of inquiry. "What is Mu?" "Who is hearing?" Our ancestors advise us to summon up great doubt. That means that doubt is there, all by itself, in your mind.

Killing Time

Yамамото Gемpō Rōshi[6] used to say, "There is no murder worse than the killing of time." He devoted an entire *teishō*[7] to this topic, reading aloud from the crime section of the newspaper. So-and-so knifed his wife and children. So-and-so ran amok at his workplace. After each item, he would repeat his theme, "There is no murder worse than the killing of time." Indeed. Let's make that our theme as well.

Light

In "The Tables Turned," Wordsworth wrote:

> Hark! How sweet the throstle sings,
> He too is no mean preacher.
> Come forth into the light of things,
> Let nature be your teacher.

"Throstle" is the old word for "thrush." What are "things" that give light? The bell, the clapper, the thrush, your thought. Their light is your light.

Ground Your Practice

YOUR PRACTICE is to make true what has always been real. You get nowhere if you sit there brooding about what a wretched specimen you are. It has always been a fact that you are true son or daughter of the Buddha. Ground your practice there and forget about what you are or might be. "What is Mu? What is Mu?"

Do Not Kill

THE DHARMA[8] is pure and simple. "Do not kill." Denial of this truth can be convoluted and complex. "Git along little doggie," chants the cowboy affectionately on the way to the slaughterhouse. "Do your patriotic duty," advises the leader on this or that side of a war. Come on! Start at the beginning. Killing is killing. Build your case there and make your presentation there, if you have the fortitude.

Teaching Yourself

ONE OF MY teacher friends cautions his students, "When you do *zazen*,[9] try 'A' way. If 'A' way doesn't work, try 'B' way." I bow to the wisdom of his words. I am not really your teacher. You must teach yourself. As far as practice goes, you are not your neighbor. What works for her might not work for you. What works for you now may not work for you next year. Keep it open.

It Is to Laugh

THE DREAM we call practice allows us to laugh. I first got acquainted with this phenomenon in Japanese monasteries. It seemed as though whenever the master opened his mouth it was to crack a joke. Gempō Rōshi grew up in a family of farm laborers whose language was of the earth. His jokes were simply outrageous. The monks laughed until they wept, and they had to fish in their sleeves for a tissue. Students who can't laugh can't dream with the sangha. They are just faking it. Let yourself go—that's what the practice is about, after all.

The Domain of Integrity

THE DEEPER our practice, the clearer truth becomes. At the source we touch the simple domain of integrity. The opposite of practice brings forth the complicated place of justification. You hear the inevitable, "What I really meant was . . . blah blah blah."

The Perfection of Character

ZAZEN IS NOT self-improvement. All these self-improvement workshops are really ego-improvement workshops. When Yamada Rōshi said, "The practice of Zen is the perfection of character," he didn't mean you correct it. He meant that body and mind fall away, and the sparkling gemstone of character stands forth pristine.

As You Are

OVER AND OVER the master assures you, "You are all right to the very bottom." This is not an assurance that beneath all your differences and peculiarities you will finally reach something called "Buddhahood." It means that your differences and peculiarities mark your Buddhahood as you are—a worthy son or daughter of Shakyamuni himself.

Long-Lost Home

Nyogen Senzaki Sensei[10] frequently quoted his teacher Shaku Sōen Zenji,[11] "Zazen is not a difficult task. It is a way to lead you to your long-lost home." Indeed. I would add that it is a way to lead you to the life your human nature anticipates.

Yourself as an Instrument

You are always establishing your practice. As soon as you notice that your mind is straying: "Mu" or "one . . . two . . . three." It's simple—very exacting, very demanding. It's also properly humbling. It becomes an exercise, as though you were learning an instrument.

Faults and Weaknesses

You are probably all too aware of your faults and weaknesses. You get angry and you are lazy. But really, faults and weaknesses are just pejorative words for qualities of character. You have faults as the Earth has faults—lines along which you expand and contract. Right Perspective is the ninth step on the Eightfold Path.[12]

Be Yourself

THE BUDDHA gave up austerities and moved on to a form of zazen. He set a fine example. You too must give up being hard on yourself and let "Mu" take over. Zazen challenges you to be yourself. It's okay to be human. The Buddha was naturally a man of great attainment. You too can be your own best person.

Essential Emptiness

THE SANSKRIT SUTRAS Zen inherited from India include the collection called the *Prajñā Pāramitā*, "Perfection of Wisdom."[13] The *Heart Sutra* and the *Vimalakirti
Sutra*[14] belong in this category. Their fundamental message is *Shunyatā,* the essential emptiness of everything.
Unless you think and conduct yourself from this position, you are not yet squared away.

Make It Clear

THE ZEN TEACHER Seikan Hasegawa said, "A *kōan*[15] is a point to be made clear."[16] That's correct. It is not associative. "The sound of one hand" is not "The sound of one hand clapping." "Mu" is not nothingness. "The one who hears sounds" is not listening to the thrush. Over and over, the master brings you back to the point.

The *Heart Sutra*

THE *HEART SUTRA* is a succinct presentation of Zen realization.[17] "Form is emptiness / emptiness is form" is the sutra's heart in turn. Ask your teacher what it means. If he or she starts explaining, then you walk out. The heart of Zen is not a matter of explanation. You are responsible for keeping the practice clean and pure.

How'm I Doing?

MOST BEGINNING Zen students are preoccupied with questions about how they are doing. I remember asking Nakagawa Sōen Rōshi[18] where I would be in terms of the Ten Ox Herding Pictures, a representation of progress on the Buddha way.[19] He said very kindly, "You are ripening." He might more accurately (and ruthlessly) have said that I wasn't yet on the chart, and my question took me further away.

The Lesser Vehicle

In the *Vimalakirti Sutra* we read the words, "Why do you seek to arouse the aspiration of your students by using the Lesser Vehicle?"[20] Well, the terms "Lesser" and "Greater" pander to the pejorative, and we don't need them. I would ask, "Why do you seek to arouse the aspiration of your students by encouraging self-improvement when fundamentally there isn't any enduring self to begin with?"

Get Serious

OUR BRIEF SUNDAY meetings are easy to sit through. Before you know it, the *Ino*[21] strikes the bell for our closing sutras—we are having tea, and heading home. It is easy to forget that one period of zazen is enough, one breath is enough.

The Meaning of *Jukai*

TO BE HUMAN is to be humane. The two words are the same, as the Oxford English Dictionary tells us. Etymology thus explicates the sacred, for the word "humane" bears meanings that take us to the depths of the Dharma. With the training, ceremony, and ongoing practice of *Jukai*,[22] we vow to realize our humane nature and its responsibilities. Our *rakusu*[23] are reminders of the sacred nature of the humanity we share. They remind us of our ancestors who pass their realization of humane nature on to us.

Book II

Seeing and Hearing

WHEN HE WAS in college, my son volunteered at the Hawaii Center for the Deaf and Blind. He observed that deaf students seemed to be more handicapped than the blind. In Zen literature seeing and hearing are both emphasized, but somehow hearing gets more attention. Bassui asked, "Who is it now that hears sounds?"[24]

The Shorter *Kannon Sutra*

THE *KANNON SUTRA FOR ETERNAL LIFE* [25] is the *Heart Sutra* in the realm of thinking. Its last two lines are its own heart: "Thought after thought arise in the mind; thought after thought are not separate from mind." When we recite this sutra in Sino-Japanese, we risk missing its meaning. We may miss its intimacy and its complementarity.

The Impact of Truth

CHANYUE GUANXIU was a master in the tenth century and is remembered particularly for his "Suggestions for Disciples," which Senzaki Sensei translated in *Buddhism and Zen*. One of the suggestions was, "Modesty is the foundation of all the virtues. Let your neighbors find you before you make yourself known to them."[26] A Diamond Sangha student told me it was this passage that awakened him to the possibilities of Zen practice.

Six Essentials

1. THERE IS a difference between Zhaozhou[27] as a historical person and Zhaozhou as one who is teaching. (He will live 120 years—that's plenty of time for you to learn.)
2. There is a difference between a kōan as an artifact and a kōan as a presentation. (Who is hearing that thrush singing so urgently in the guava grove?)
3. There is a difference between waiting and "mustering body and mind." (What is happening?)
4. There is a difference between going through the motions and making it personal. (What is your real name?)
5. There is a difference between opinion and truth. (What is the time right now?)
6. What does "Mu" mean to you? What does "body and mind drop away" mean to you? Show me!

Me to You

Gasshō is the Japanese equivalent of the Sanskrit *anjali*. It is the greeting, palm to palm, found among people throughout Asia, from the Dalai Lama to the Singhalese peasant, from the Pakistani weaver to the Japanese business executive. One palm is you and the other is me, and we are together. Gasshō has universal appeal—my Tongan American caregivers respond to it with a clear grasp of its intimate message.

The Dōjō

Dōjō is a Japanese word that means "Dharma hall." It designates the room or building where monks, nuns, and laypeople do zazen. Dōjō translates the Sanskrit *bodhimanda,* the spot under the Bodhi tree where the Buddha had his great realization. The corner in your home where you do zazen is your dōjō. You bow with your hands palm to palm when you enter and exit that corner. Your cushions are your dōjō, and you bow to them as well. You yourself are your dōjō, and you venerate yourself. Thus the Dharma takes its rightful place in our daily lives.

Enticement to Live

GEMPŌ RŌSHI RETIRED as master of Ryūtakuji monastery in 1951 at the age of eighty-six, after teaching there since 1915. He lived out the remaining ten years of his life in a hermitage attended by the monk Suzuki Sōchū, who later became master of Ryūtakuji himself. The old man never had much of an appetite, and he lost even that in his last years. Despite his master's lack of interest in food, Sōchū Oshō[28] kept him alive. He was a fine cook, and had prepared delicacies for his old teacher at the monastery for many years. Finally, however, his enticements ran out. The old man just stopped eating, and died at ninety-six. It was time to go at last.

Guanyin

THE HONOLULU ACADEMY of Arts, one of the finest small art museums anywhere, was established when I was about ten years old. I would ride my bicycle especially to see the Guanyin,[29] a life-size Song period figure on display there. The collection was limited in those days, and she reposed in the mudrā[30] of Royal Ease alone at one end of a large room. There are other exhibits in the room now, but she continues to hold forth in the same place, more beautiful than ever. I had no idea who she was back then, and now that I know something about her iconography she is an even greater figure of mystery.

The Dharma

WHEN I WAS a young student of Zen in Japan, I haunted bookstores in the Kanda district of Tokyo in search of books related to my practice. I would get lost in the legal section of the shops, as the graph for "Dharma" is the same as the graph for "law." This makes sense, for the two meanings are the same. "Singing and dancing are the voice of the law," as Hakuin Ekaku Zenji wrote.[31]

Schiller's Creator

YAMADA RŌSHI used to play music on his phonograph for us when we joined him for tea, following our evening *dokusan*.[32] Once when the fourth movement of Beethoven's Ninth Symphony drew to a close with its burst of chorus of Schiller's "Ode to Joy," he pointed out that Schiller was hardly the equal of Beethoven. The Rōshi rumbled a bit of the lyrics to the Ode, first in the German original, and then in English: "Do you sense the Creator's world? / Seek him above the starry canopy, / Above the stars he must live." "Ah," exclaimed the Rōshi. "His Creator was certainly far away!"

Yakuseki

YAKUSEKI, meaning "medicine stone," is the Japanese word for "supper" that is used in Zen monasteries. Classical Buddhist monks do not eat after noon, but in the northern clime of the Mahayana, it would be unhealthy to fast for this third meal of the day. The medicine stone is heated in Asian medicine and placed on an ailing stomach. In the monastery, the leftovers from breakfast and the noon meal are heated with a bit of miso and served without sutras. It is *yakuseki*, technically not a meal, and thus the old strictures are unbroken.

The Raft Is the Shore

A NUMBER of scholars at Western universities have written about Zen Buddhism. Some of their studies have been pretty bad, and others are pretty good. Dale S. Wright, professor of Religious Studies at Occidental College, and his *Philosophical Meditations on Zen Buddhism* put them all in the shade. To mix metaphors: "Even the most productive fishermen get hungry again."[33] Once and for all, the notion that the raft is just a means to reach the other shore is laid to rest.

The Mountains and Rivers Sesshin

ZEN IN THE WEST is faithful to its antecedents, or else it is faithless one way or another. The formal Mountains and Rivers campout is both faithful and innovative. It is an outdoor sesshin[34] practice that can be traced historically to experiments by Gary Snyder and his friends at the Ring of Bone Zendo[35] in the Sierra Foothills back in the early '80s, and refined there and by other Diamond Sangha folks in the U.S. and Australia. The sesshin can be scheduled for just a couple of days or for an entire week. Participants hike and camp in the wilderness, in silence as much as possible. Dokusan is held outdoors in the evenings and early mornings. I'm sure our ancestors are exclaiming, "Now why didn't we try that!"

Vacancy!

WHEN SŌEN RŌSHI ascended to the "high seat" and became the master at Ryūtakuji, there was a huge party at the monastery. People who came from afar stayed overnight so the monks had to double up. The Rōshi and I slept in the same room, and in the middle of the night he wakened me when he shouted in his sleep, in English: "Vacancy! Vacancy! Wonderful vacancy!"

Bishop Ditch

THE *TSUREZUREGUSA* ("*Random Grasses*") by Yoshida
Kenkō is a medieval Japanese precedent for these miniatures.[36] It consists of 243 entries, varying in length from
a single line to a few pages, including the story of Bishop
Nettle Tree. It seems that the Bishop was a bad-tem-
pered and unpopular village cleric who had a big nettle
tree in his front garden. Angered by his nickname, he
had the tree cut down. He was then known as "Bishop
Stump." Incensed even further, he had the stump dug
up. He was then known as "Bishop Ditch."

Folk Stories of Zen

KŌANS ARE the folk stories of Zen, the fairy tales, the myths, the legends. They are deeply instructive and transformative, and they are destroyed by explanation. Mu is not "no" or "nothingness" any more than Little Red Riding Hood is a cautionary tale about seduction. You respect the needs of children to process fairy tales on their own. Likewise Zen students must process kōans themselves without getting an explanation from the master.

Zen Study

"LIKE THE SKY, you lean on nothing." This was the last line of a hymn of praise to Shakyamuni Buddha by the Bejeweled Accumulation.[37] Some people miss such joyous exposition because they limit their formal practice to the preliminaries of work on their cushions, and are not able to practice leaning on nothing in their daily lives. They are like the elementary school student whose education is just a series of workbooks.

The Buddha Dharma

ONCE I TOOK Sōen Rōshi to visit a Chinese Buddhist temple in Honolulu. The resident priest was very cordial, but he spoke little English. The Rōshi was not much more fluent, but he found a sutra book in Chinese, and the two priests recited the *Heart Sutra* together. Of course their pronunciations were a little different, but the ideographs were the same in the two languages. Word by word they chanted, ending triumphantly together.

The Beginning of Practice

YASUTANI HAKU'UN RŌSHI[38] hosted a dinner party for
the sangha at Kamakura to honor one of his senior students who had completed his formal kōan study. I am
not a proponent of such commemorations, but one thing
the Rōshi said in his address about the honoree made it
worthwhile. "Now," he said, "his practice begins." We
who were stuck on Mu rolled our eyes as we stole looks
at each other, but now I offer incense and bow in gratitude to my old teacher.

The Exacting Master

WHEN PEOPLE ASK what they can bring me, I am challenged to my very essence and respond, "Bring Zhaozhou out from the shadows!" Or I might reply, "Thank you. I am looking for a sensible man or woman." Am I too exacting?

Improvised Practice

THE FIRST MEETING place of what became the Honolulu Diamond Sangha was the Aitken living room in the
suburb of Kuliouou in the fall of 1959. We sat on sofa
cushions and chairs and timed our zazen with a Pyrex
bowl and a wooden spoon. Our clappers were salvaged
from a construction site next door. Still, we tried to see
to it that the way of Bodhidharma[39] was not makeshift.

"Beginner's Mind"

SUZUKI SHUNRYŪ RŌSHI[40] gave the old Zen expression "Beginner's Mind" a lasting place in American Zen. It is part of the title of his book in English, *Zen Mind, Beginner's Mind*, and is likewise the name of the San Francisco Zen Center building, "Beginner's Mind Temple." It is also the name of my practice and yours.

The Rich Ambiguity

SOME PEOPLE USE the word "retreat" for the Sino-Japanese term *sesshin*. This is too bad. Yamada Rōshi would explain that sesshin has three meanings: "to touch the mind, to receive the mind, and to convey the mind." Using "retreat" for this rich ambiguity dumbs down the practice. People who know this and still say "retreat" don't belong here.

Hush Hush

YAMADA RŌSHI and I had not met for a while, and he brought news from Kamakura. He reported that one of our friends had inoperable cancer, adding, "Of course she doesn't know." Of course? Of course, the patient really knows, after all, and pretends not to. Ultimately our friend died, and she and her family missed an important chance for intimacy.

Maezumi Rōshi

I LED my first sesshin as an independent teacher in the summer of 1974. To commemorate the occasion, my students presented me with Zenkei Shibayama's *Zen Comments on the Mumonkan*, which was then just published. My delight turned to chagrin. I couldn't understand it. Taking my wife Anne by the hand, I fled to Los Angeles to consult with Maezumi Taizan Rōshi,[41] who very kindly set me on my feet. The process took many months, and I am eternally grateful.

The Old Teacher

THE TITLE *Rōshi* means "Old Teacher." It is an informal term of endearment and affection extended to the master by his or her students. Yamada Rōshi translated it as "Old Boss." It is not a title like "professor" in academia. It is a mistake to say, for example, "His master made him a Rōshi." In truth the master says, "Our eyes are the same," and the students take it from there. Be that as it may, after all these years, I've concluded that the personal name of the new teacher is the best title.

Women in Zen

ONE OF THE ELEMENTS of Zen and Chan which thankfully did not survive movement from India, Japan, and China to the Western world is a pig-headed attitude toward women. It was not built into the practice and was basically a cultural prejudice. I love the account in the *Vimalakirti Sutra* of a goddess who changed Shariputra into a goddess and herself into Shariputra, and generally showed him up.[42]

Itadakimas

ITADAKIMAS IS AN important word in the Japanese language. Literally, it means, "I place this over my head," and is translated as "I humbly receive." It is the blessing which all Japanese, from the day laborer to the prime minister, intone before a meal, even a snack. It is the saving grace of Japanese culture.

Upright Livelihood

"UPRIGHT LIVELIHOOD" is a step on the Eightfold Path. The Buddha warned that the job of guarding prisoners is not upright. Incredibly, there are two million people or more in prison in the United States today. It would take massive deviation from the Eightfold Path to keep the system going. No wonder people call Buddhism unrealistic.

Zen and Psychology

MANY ZEN STUDENTS and even a few teachers think Zen is a kind of psychology. This is a little like thinking that persimmons are a kind of banana. The Zen master is more like a flea than he or she is like a psychologist. More like a cool breeze. More like a mountain peak. I am not exaggerating or being fanciful.

The Snow Man

WALLACE STEVENS ends his poem "The Snow Man" with the lines, "Nothing that is not there, / And the nothing that is."[43] When I studied American literature in college, the instructor said, "This is a kind of nihilism." If so, the definition of nihilism needs expanding.

Upright Speech

ONE OF THE GEMS of modern Hawaiian wisdom is "Don't talk stink." Sōen Rōshi used to say, "Don't use rootless words." "Upright Speech" is part of the Eight-fold Path. It's easy to set these commonsense reminders to one side.

Coping with One's Mistakes

SUZUKI SHUNRYŪ RŌSHI said, "Being a Zen master means coping with one's mistakes." Indeed, and it's a pretty lonely position. If you confess to your errors, some of your good students will go away. If you don't confess, you yourself will go away. I don't wonder at the alcoholism found occasionally in sacred halls.

The Great Master

In 1958, when Anne Aitken and I were completing our final year at the Happy Valley School in Ojai, California, Sōen Rōshi visited us from Japan. We held a reception for him, and Emanuel Sherman came, wearing a Zen monk's robe. The Rōshi admired his robe, and Manny explained that it was a gift from his old teacher, Sasaki Shigetsu Rōshi,[44] in New York, before World War II. He pointed out that Shigetsu Rōshi had inscribed a brief message to go with his gift, and it was sewed into the back of a lapel. He asked Sōen Rōshi to read it for him. The Rōshi exclaimed, "Did Shigetsu Rōshi write that? What a great master he was!" Manny asked, "What does it say?" Sōen Rōshi just repeated, "What a great master!" Manny persisted, "What does it say?" The Rōshi finally intoned, "It says, 'Don't look around!'" I marvel too. The guidance of the Buddha himself is encapsulated in those three words.

Not Conventional

IN THE ZEN literature you will find a broad spectrum of seemingly unconventional human conduct used as teachings, from Ikkyū's elegant cunnilingus poems[45] to the story of the master Danxia burning a wooden image of the Buddha to keep himself warm.[46] Be careful. The message is not that anything goes. It's just that the Dharma is not something put together by Miss Manners.

Ailments of Old Age

HONG ZICHENG SAID, "The ailments of old age are really those incurred in youthful times. Weakness in one's last years is really something wrought in the prime of life. Therefore, when life is at its peak, the noble person endeavors exactingly to take full care in every way."[47] The problem with this truism is that usually by the time it rings true, it's too late.

A World Religion

SOMEONE ASKED Senzaki Sensei if Zen would become a world religion. He replied, "No, zazen is not for everyone." He never advertised his little center, and was content to live out his life as an unknown mountain mushroom, as he put it, with no roots or branches.

Important Work

I HAVE the utmost admiration for students who stick with the practice despite all kinds of adverse circumstances. Listening to their accounts of arising early and doing zazen alone every morning of the week no matter how tired they are, I recall my own diligence long ago, and I include myself in my admiration. What important work we are doing!

Yaza

Yaza, "NIGHT SITTING," is a custom in Japanese monasteries. In some it is announced as voluntary for the final night of sesshin, before the last day of sitting. In others it is practiced every night and is *de rigueur.* There are no clappers or bells. Monks sit as long as they wish and do *kinhin*[48] when they feel like it. I sat up like this at an early sesshin of the Koko An Zendo, and when Sōen Rōshi shouted in the dōjō the next morning, my voice joined his. That incident marked the moment my practice started to move at last.

Study Practice

It is important to study the Dharma in translations from the Sanskrit, Chinese, and Japanese, even if
you can't make yourself conversant in those languages.
There are also worthwhile English commentaries on the
Dharma, and there are Western writers from Shake-
speare to Wallace Stevens who know what's what clearly
and creatively. Ikkyū Sōjun Zenji said the book burner
is Māra, the Evil One, personified.[49] If your teacher says,
"Don't ever read," find yourself another teacher.

No Almighty God

BUDDHISM SPRANG from India and evolved into Zen and other sects in China, where people find inspiration in stones, clouds, cats and their fleas. The shift of Buddhism from the rich Indian views of a spiritual dimension to the down-to-earth Chinese attitude is fundamental, and modern students of Zen in the Western hemisphere must thus unlearn the notion that realization relates solely to something unworldly. To begin with there is no Almighty God.

Simone Weil

Simone Weil is one of several Western writers of interest to Zen students. She knew about the virtue of attention and frequently wrote about it. She also knew about the value of folk stories as purveyors of truth. But most of all, she took her identity with all beings seriously, even to the point of sacrificing her life to be with French peasants who were losing theirs. I light incense for you, Simone.

My Damned Mother

In the early days of my Zen practice, I had a problem with my mother. She had expressed doubt about my trustworthiness in a money matter, although it was something I had taken care of honorably. The zendo would be totally silent, everything would be supportive of good zazen, and I would sit there with the mantra, "My damned mother!" Maybe if I had been guilty I wouldn't have been so troubled. My problem was self-righteousness, after all.

What Happens after Death?

WHEN I ASKED Yamada Rōshi, "What happens after death?" he replied, "Of course there is always the phenomenal side." When that question is put to me, I say, "I don't know." I never fail to think of my old teacher. Even when I imagine that he is looking over my shoulder, I still can't respond with his answer. I really don't know but—at ninety—I'll find out soon.

The Attitude toward Dr. Suzuki

ONE OF THE many things that surprised me about Zen as it is practiced in Japanese monasteries is the general dismissal of Dr. D. T. Suzuki.[50] He was a good friend, and it took me a long time to understand this disparagement. Now I get it. *Satori*[51] or *kenshō*[52] is not a be-all and end-all experience, as you might suppose from his writings. It just marks the first realization, if that. Maezumi Rōshi often said, "I never passed my first kōan."

Zazen for the Mentally Unstable

I once asked Zenkei Shibayama Rōshi,[53] "What is zazen for the mentally unstable person?" He replied, "Zazen is for the person whose mental health is especially vigorous." I agree. It is hard enough for the hale and hearty person to stay centered. It is dangerous for unbalanced persons even to try. The silence of the dōjō can drop them into the inferno unimaginable.

Put God on the Shelf

I MET a Catholic sister in Japan who did zazen under the guidance of Yamada Rōshi. One day she asked him, "What shall I do about God?" He replied, "Put God on the shelf for a while." Wise advice! Without using any name, her sacred imperative would resolve her question.

Shin-jin Datsu Raku

ONCE LONG AGO I took part in a large Japanese Zen celebration framed as a sesshin, and confronted four masters in a formal setting. To one after the other, I asked the same question, "What is *shin-jin datsu raku*?" ("Body and mind fall away.") Each one replied, "Aw, you know about that, Aitken-san," or something similar. When I told Yamada Rōshi about this, he exclaimed, "Four of them! Terrible! Awful! Whatever happened to *shin-jin datsu raku*? Oh! There's that thrush again!"

Breath Counting

BACK IN the earliest days of the Koko An Zendo, we hosted a high Sri Lankan master for an evening. He gave a little talk and then invited questions. I asked, "How do you instruct beginners?" He answered the question with a disquisition on breath counting, exactly as we had heard from our own Japanese teachers. Now, more than forty years later, it is clear to me that breath counting is not merely for beginners. Some old-timers continue with it as their regular practice. It can lead one to an initial realization just as a kōan can.

In Charge of Nature

IN ASIA, sesshins are keyed to the seasons and named for seasonal phenomena. Haiku, the tiny Japanese verses of seventeen syllables, must have a seasonal reference, or they are not haiku. Just after World War II, daylight saving time was enforced in Japan by American authorities. When the occupation ended, the first act of the independent Japanese government was to repeal daylight saving time. Though they forget it sometimes, Japanese people know in their hearts that human beings are not in charge of nature.

Whitman and Dōgen

THE BASIC LESSON of Zen is, "Forget yourself." Even old-timers fail to apply this fundamental teaching. It may seem contradictory that the jewel of the individual can only be realized by letting it drop away. "Do I contradict myself? Very well then I contradict myself (I am large, I contain multitudes)." Walt Whitman, meet Dōgen Kigen.[54]

Beliefs

You will hear that Bodhidharma was the founder of the martial arts. That's okay. He's not around to affirm or deny. Some people believe that angels rolled away the stone that sealed the tomb of Jesus Christ. That's okay. Now if you'll excuse me, that was the bell for zazen.

The Disadvantage
of Being an Old-Timer

OLD-TIMERS IN the dōjō are at a certain disadvantage. They know what will happen next, and their minds can stray into the future. The newcomer doesn't know what is going on, and is thus obliged to focus on the immediate. How can old-timers be encouraged not to think about what will be? This is the challenge.

Dangerous Work

SOON AFTER I was authorized to teach, Sōen Rōshi asked me, "How are you getting on with your dangerous work?" I had no idea what he was talking about, but I soon learned. Students are sometimes at play where the moonlight of wisdom is indeed lunar. This teaching of etymology should give the master pause.

The Way of Yao

DUNGSHAN LIANGJIE[55] advises us to make the way of Yao our own. Yao was an emperor in mythological times. He encouraged homemakers to sing to their little ones as they helped them dress for their day. He encouraged merchants to dance in the market and artisans to weave imaginative designs at their looms. How else can we enjoy our stint of humanity!

No Zazen for Children

I USED TO THINK that twenty-five might be the right age to begin Zen practice. I'm beginning to think that thirty-five might be better. In any case, zazen is not for children. Dr. Kazue Yamada, the Rōshi's widow, was quite firm about this. I can hear her now: "Don't let them even try. Send them outside to play."

A Loaded Word

We venerate the Three Treasures
And are thankful for this meal—
The work of many people
And the sharing of other forms of life.

THIS BRIEF, INFORMAL, mealtime gatha probably orig-
inated in the San Francisco Zen Center. I have heard
that the last line once read: "And the suffering of other
forms of life," but "suffering" became "sharing" as the
gatha moved out to other centers. We are not responsible for suffering, now are we!

Dumbing Down

USING THE WORD "lecture" for the Sino-Japanese term *teishō* is another act of dumbing down the Dharma. While teishō can mean "lecture," its etymology and its implication are more like "a presentation of the shout." Leave the term untranslated and you will be faithful to the way of the teishō. It is the meaning itself, rather than an exposition on the meaning.

Déjà Vu

Déjà vu is a relatively common experience, and is often dismissed as a quirk of memory, but it has an emotional content that lingers. It opens the door to the otherwise hidden world of coincidence. Two people fall in love and express the feeling that they must have known each other in a previous life. You discover your intended vocation. Déjà vu can be realization itself as old Zhaozhou makes his point at last:

> If you pass the barrier you will not only see Zhaozhou intimately, but you will go hand in hand with all the masters of the past. Seeing with the same eyes, hearing with the same ears.[56]

Be Decent

THERE IS an eleventh Grave Precept,[57] "Be decent." We tend to limit our use of the words "decent" and "decency" to their derivative meanings and to relegate them to stupid convention. The primary use of the words refers to action and attitudes in the context of their fundamental circumstances. Superficial social convention might be altogether indecent.

First Reasons

BACK IN THE early Maui Zendo days, a family had a flat tire on the road past our place. They knocked on our door seeking help, and stayed six months. This might be a better story if one of them turned out to be a long-term student who is still practicing with us, but as it stands it illustrates the point that your initial reasons for Zen practice don't matter at all. You can start wherever you are. Zen is a repair kit you can use to fix the basic problem that awaits human resolution. You can open it and use the tools on the road or in your own garage.

This Very Body

In his "Song of Zazen," Hakuin Zenji wrote, "This very place is the Lotus Land, / This very body the Buddha."[58] We recite this passage without a second thought, yet there is nothing more radical and presumptuous in the myriad expressions of the Dharma. How can I say that the social morass around me is Heaven itself? How can I say that this very shithead is enlightened?

Enlightenment

AT AN INFORMAL MEETING with us at Koko An, a monk
from Japan asked, "How many people here have enlightenment? Raise your hands." We just sat there, stunned.
Yet some of us make the same outrageous mistake. How
many of us aim for realization? Ha! Ha! Come on!

Awareness of Time

TIME IS the measurement we impose on our existence, and if in your formal practice you remain aware of the passage of the periods of zazen, you are not giving yourself a chance to let your body and mind drop away. It doesn't matter if you forget the clock. Or to put it in another way, it matters very much indeed.

Circumambulation

CIRCUMAMBULATION, the practice of walking around something sacred, is found in all cultures, from Zanzibar to Scotland. It is almost always done clockwise, the direction the shadow of the sun moves around the sundial. Only in Black Mass and in the practice of Bon in Tibet do you find widdershins, counterclockwise circumambulation. I suspect that the Bon ritual serves as defense against the influence of Varjayana just next door. In any case, the worldwide acknowledgment of the sun and its path is our guide in even the smallest details of our zendo ritual. It is the primordial way.

The Jewels

In 1950 I lived in Wahiawa, a town in central Oʻahu, and Claude DuTeil was our Episcopal minister. He was young and very popular. Another well-liked man in town died suddenly of chicken pox at the age of thirty-eight. We were all stricken. We gathered in the church for the funeral and the widow appeared at the last moment, her face drawn but unveiled. Then Claude came forth from the wings. Dressed in his formal robes, he paced slowly, intoning, "I am the way, the truth, and the light." He seemed transformed. I was transformed as well, and felt deeply in touch with myself. The words of *The Book of Common Prayer*, like the words in other sacred texts across the world, are jewels of humankind. We burnish them in their settings as we intone them.

Thomas Traherne (1636–1674)

TRAHERNE'S *Centuries of Meditation* was unknown until it was discovered in manuscript in a bookstall in 1888, and then published in modern English in 1908. This is perhaps its most celebrated passage:

> You never know the world aright till the Sea floweth in your Veins, till you are Clothed with the Heavens, and Crowned with the Stars; And perceive yourself to be the Sole Heir of the Whole World; And more then so, because Men are in it who are every one Sole Heirs, as well as you. Till you are intimately Acquainted with that Shady Nothing out of which this World was made; Till your spirit filleth the whole World and the Stars are your Jewels; Till you love Men so as to Desire their Happiness with a thirst equal to the zeal of your own.[59]

Book III

The Myth of Sisyphus

I have found the works of Albert Camus difficult to read, but I'm persuaded by his fable, "The Myth of Sisyphus,"[60] that he could be simple and profound. You will recall that in Homer's account of the myth, Sisyphus is doomed to spend eternity in Hell, rolling a boulder up a mountain, only to have it slip from his grasp just as he is about to reach the top, and then to repeat his task again and again forever. Camus gives riches to Homer, and it is the sentence at the end of his essay that convinced me: "The struggle itself toward the heights is enough to fill a man's heart." Indeed! Ask any master worthy of his title about this.

The Middle Initial

My GRANDFATHER, the astronomer Robert Grant Aitken, once remarked to me, "I spent the entire afternoon confirming the middle initial of William Herschel, the British astronomer. I suppose you might think I was wasting my time." I didn't think so then, and I remember him now as I confirm a Dharma name, then transliterate it from the Hepburn transcription to the Wade-Giles, and finally to the Pinyin. I am grateful to Grandfather for his genes.

Danger Man

I MET a young Asian man who had had remarkably good training in religious practice with an excellent master, but who had fallen under the sway of a subsequent teacher who convinced him that he was a perfect guru who could do no wrong. So with overweening confidence in an unfamiliar Western setting, the young man made terrible mistakes, and created havoc at every turn. He was what local folks in Hawai'i call a "danger man."

Gratitude

ARIGATAI is another significant Japanese term. Literally it means "I'm unworthy." It is an expression of gratitude. When viewing a particularly beautiful sunset, one exclaims, *"Arigatai né!"* "Doesn't that give rise to gratitude!" The derivative *arigatō* is universal—"thank you"— one of the first expressions the infant learns.

Guidelines

JOHN KEATS admonished his friend and fellow poet Percy Bysshe Shelley, "Load every rift with ore."[61] Logan Pearsall Smith apparently admonished himself in his composition of his *Trivia* books to let each entry have a beginning, a middle, and an end—and to avoid repeating a word in a sequence of nine, except articles and for emphasis.[62] Keats and Smith keep me straight; now it's up to me to follow through.

Love Never Faileth

WHEN I WAS a boy I attended church with my parents. The sermons sailed over my head unattended. I would make my eyes go out of focus and the minister could be young like me. My attention would stray to St. Paul's words inscribed in gold letters high above the pulpit, "Love Never Faileth." "What does that mean?" I wondered. To this day, I can't put it into other words.

The Drunk

ONE SUNDAY MORNING in my boyhood a drunk tottered into church during the sermon. In those days of Prohibition, people in Hawai'i drank "swipes," made from fermented pineapples and raisins. It was a smelly drink, and this man stank to high heaven. He had the undivided attention of the congregation. He wandered out again, and then returned. This time an usher escorted him out for good. Afterwards I asked my dad, "What happened to that drunken man?" He said, "I think the usher drove him home." It was my lesson in decency for that Sunday.

Love

"LOVE" IS an overused word that we find in countless everyday usages, from comic opera to postage stamps. Yet it remains important in pillow talk, in interaction with children, and among close friends in correspondence. It is your responsibility and mine to limit its usage and thus keep it alive.

Prevalence of Gays

I suppose that homosexuality is as widespread in Japan as it is anywhere. Gays and lesbians there flourish in the artistic demimonde, but are not acknowledged in the mainstream, where they are married off willy-nilly. Sometimes they turn to the abbot of a nearby temple for counseling. After a couple of months in this role, Sōen Rōshi remarked to me, "I had no idea that homosexuality was so prevalent"—or, I might add now, how social denial is causing such extensive and excruciating misery.

The Midway Rail

In what seems like an earlier incarnation, I worked in construction on Midway Island in the North Pacific Ocean in 1940. I was enchanted by Midway Rails, tiny wingless birds the size of a chick that would run around our garbage cans. One of our fellows was an amateur ornithologist. He caught one, killed it, and mounted its remains. I objected, but it turns out that civilization was too much for the little beings. The Midway Rail is now extinct, and maybe my friend's specimen is our only reminder.

The Naming of Children

I was once acquainted with Egerton Allerton Throckmorton. He called himself "Bill." At age thirteen he ran away from home and joined the circus. I heard that when still a young man, he was killed in Africa as a soldier of fortune. Maybe I err in reading cause and effect here, but it could be a cautionary tale. In any case, when you name your child, you set a certain train of karma in motion. How will it play out?

The Illegal Annexation

In 1993, the United States government officially apologized for illegally annexing the Hawaiian kingdom in 1898. The Hawaiian people and their friends aren't sure what to do now. Maybe we can learn from the Singing Revolution in Estonia, Latvia, and Lithuania that helped to bring down the Soviet Union a while back. The beautiful songs of our last sovereign Queen Liliuokalani, are now available.[63] We could sing them together as one big community every Sunday afternoon sitting on the grass at Iolani Palace—and see what happens.

Son of a Famous Man Syndrome

My father, Robert Thomas Aitken, suffered from "Son of a Famous Man" syndrome, though in his time we didn't have the affliction identified. He was Robert Aitken, just like his father, who was a prominent astronomer. Dad completed his doctoral dissertation in anthropology, and was on a train to Philadelphia to defend it. Riding along he was looking it over. He decided it was no good, and threw it out the window. I suspect he was responding to a little voice that was whispering, "Watch out! You might succeed!"

The World of Make-Believe

As CHILDREN we live in the world of make-believe, Once Upon a Time, and Goldilocks and the Three Bears, not to mention witches and goblins. Today make-believe is the world we know as teenagers and adults. Witches and goblins seem to have the upper hand. We don't know we are making believe—they encroach on our world and actually endanger it. How to cope is the overriding question.

Step'um

I USED TO VISIT an inmate at the old Oahu Prison. I would line up with the families outside the prison and wait to be shown into the reception area. Once I stood waiting near a young mother and her four-year-old son. He noticed a bug on the sidewalk, and squatted down to watch it. He looked up at his mother and said, "Lookit the bug." "Step'um," she said coldly. He squashed it manfully with his foot. Thereby, I imagine, he learned a lesson similar to ones his father had learned at his age.

The Noble Cause

My GREAT-GRANDFATHER, Robert Thomas Aitken, had a resonant bass voice, in keeping with his Welsh heritage. In the American Civil War, he was a captain in an Illinois regiment. On the march, he would sing the verses of the Battle Hymn of the Republic, "Mine eyes have seen the glory of the coming of the Lord"—and the entire regiment would join in the chorus, "Glory, glory, hallelujah!" The Civil War was a noble cause, but wait a minute! It is also known as the "War Between the States." The difference in nomenclature marks a bitter contention that, at this writing, still rages in courts and legislative halls across the land.

Choosing Your Battle

TRUE PARENTS KNOW how to choose their battles. Patience and trust in the possibility of self-correction will often do the trick. If Mother says too often, "Gwendolyn, go pick up your messy room," Gwendolyn will eventually be changing her name to Suzie. If the atmosphere gets too oppressive, Gwen's defenses can solidify, and the wrong thing will somehow become all right. Prisons are full of people who harbor such a notion.

Overhead Wiring

Pictures of New York City in the late nineteenth century show a veritable jungle of overhead wires. Technology has advanced a little since then and most of those wires are now unnecessary or underground. We still have them, however, and Tenth Avenue in our own Pālolo Valley in Honolulu is a mess. A hundred years from now, everything will be digital, views will be unimpeded, and the whole city will be beautiful. That is assuming that people will be around to make this possible.

All Beings Are Sick

VIMALAKIRTI SAID to Manjushrī, "I am sick because all living beings are sick."[64] You don't have to be an incredibly wise Bodhisattva to appreciate his words. You can just turn your ordinary intelligence to progressive periodicals to learn what you already know: self-aggrandizement is the illness—in big selves like nations, and in small, individual selves. Foremost among the symptoms is a wall for nations and pathologically thick skin for its folks.

What Works for You?

CAREER, FAMILY, Zen practice—each one affects the others. The proper proportions of the mix for one student will not be the same as they are for another. This is not a dilemma. Choose your mix, and make it work. Maybe after a wholehearted try it will become evident that the arrangement needs adjustment—maybe just a tweak, maybe something radical. Keep yourself open. What will work in the bigger picture of your responsibility?

Our Elders

OUR ELDERS ARE not just old folks who inherited good genes and have the wherewithal for medical care. Our elders are also those who somehow survived here and there in little pockets of ancient culture amid the compulsion to cover the Earth with macadam and cement. It is essential that we listen to them. The people we have almost obliterated can save us, after all.

Obedient Objects

THE SCIENTIST whose experiment does not work out might complain more or less good-humoredly about the "innate perversity of inanimate objects." That may be a mildly amusing reaction, but it's not correct. It's the scientist who is perverse. Objects always follow the law of their being. Even if the outcome will destroy the human race, the object will be faithful.

Kenneth Rexroth

WHO READS Kenneth Rexroth these days? But surely he'll be rediscovered:

> Man is a social animal;
> That is, top dog of a slave state.[65]

Rexroth was one of a few. For him, to know animals and birds was to love them. He knew the meaning of dominion, and cried out when that knowledge was violated.

Remembered in Museums

As A BOY I read about the complete extermination of the original people of Tasmania. I remember reflecting that I would find such a land to be barren—and I couldn't live in such a place. There I was in Hawai'i, oblivious of a history of desecration that differed only in degree from the loss in Tasmania. There I was in the United States, where entire flesh-and-blood cultures are remembered only in museums. It is all too easy to be oblivious to one's own involvement.

The Listening Project

THE FELLOWSHIP of Reconciliation instituted the Listening Project during the Yugoslavian conflict. A couple of FOR members would settle into the living room of partisans of one side or another, turn on a tape recorder, and just let their hosts talk. The transcripts would be edited without comment into booklets, and released into the market. It was startling to find the similarities in the various sides. The head of the house would begin, "Let me give you a lesson in history"—and he would launch into a story of abuse from the thirteenth or fourteenth century.

Sixty Miles an Hour

ONCE WHEN my father was involved in research on the island of Tubuai back in 1920, he entertained his subjects with an account of the automobile, which they had never seen. "It will go sixty miles in an hour," he said. There was a stunned silence. Finally an old-timer spoke up. "You're a liar," he said. "If you go sixty miles in an hour, you'll run off the island!" It was Dad's turn to be silent.

Truth-telling

In the old days of the Maui Zendo there were members who felt that they must be "honest." They would tell other members exactly what they thought of them. They would feel better afterwards but everybody else would feel terrible. This kind of truth-telling can have the opposite effect, however. Judiciously expressed, it can save us all.

At Waimanalo Pier

WHEN I WAS a boy, our family spent many Sundays at Waimanalo Beach. It had a fishing pier in those days, and our dad tried to get my brother Malcolm and me to use it as a diving platform. Both of us kids were afraid of the waves, especially me. Dad taunted me, saying that I had a broad yellow streak down my back. I failed him and myself, and when at last we drove home, the misery in our silent ride was palpable. My message to parents is that your kid gets enough taunting at school on weekdays. Sunday should be a day of sympathy and support.

Wrong as Hell

THE ARCHBISHOP Desmond Tutu has said, "This is a moral universe; right and wrong matter."[66] Indeed, and not just the universe but its human beings as well. We are all of us intrinsically moral, and we know that right and wrong matter. Witness the war veterans who suffer post-traumatic stress disorder. This often happens after the stress of killing—stress at the very core of being human. War is wrong as hell!

The Fragrant Emperor

Personal decisions often rest on the frail reed of strategy: What is best for me? ME! ME! ME! National decisions have the same basis: ME! ME! ME!—writ large. It doesn't work. The stench that pervades the system can be traced to rotting bodies. Yet there is a way to purify this mess. Any nursery school teacher will tell us to be decent. If we listen, if we truly hear, then for sure the emperor will stand forth in resplendent robes, bejeweled and perfumed. We will dance in the streets while clowns cavort around on stilts.

Book IV

The Mountain Stream

I VISITED ARGENTINA in 1989, and on my return I stopped in Guatemala by arrangement with my friend Joe Gorin. He had just finished his contract with Peace Brigades International and was free to guide me. On our rickety bus ride at midnight from the highlands to the airport at the end of my eleven-day tour, the road was narrow and steep. The headlights failed soon after we began our descent, and the driver was obliged to depend entirely on a flashlight held by his assistant. There we were, plunging through the dark. I was in the throes of pneumonia, and my hallucination was fixed on a shallow mountain stream flowing over pretty little stones. We survived our dangerous ride, and that vision of a mountain stream with its pretty stones continues to sustain me. It flows on and on, at some level, deep in my zazen.

The *Palaka* Shirt

THE *PALAKA* SHIRT is a significant part of modern Hawaiian culture. The word is a transliteration of the English "plaid." It is the blue-and-white checked cotton shirt that was issued to plantation workers in early days as a protection against sharp sugarcane and pineapple leaves. The plantations and the suffering of the workers are in the past now, but old-timers continue to wear *palaka* shirts by way of saying, "We don't forget."

The Eightfold Path

WHEN I WAS a youngster I went with my Sunday School class on a field trip to a Buddhist temple. The priest of the temple spoke to us about the Eightfold Path. I thought I had never been so bored in all the years of my young life. I would not in the wide world have supposed that one day I would become a friend and colleague of that same priest, the Venerable Ernest Hunt, and I would make the Eightfold Path my own inspiration.

The Empty Space

As my son Tom was researching the topic of secrets and closeted behavior, he came across the story of a Jewish woman in Nazi Germany who hid her faith and survived. She established a network of Aryan friends, married, and started a family. The war ended, but she felt that she still could not reveal her religious faith. As time went on, her daughter fell in love with the son of an Orthodox rabbi, and they were married. Thus her daughter filled in the empty space that circumstances and she herself had created.[67]

Saint Andrew

ST. FRANCIS OF ASSISI is the patron saint of animals and birds, and once a year he is honored in a special mass dedicated to dogs and cats and horses. Less celebrated is St. Andrew, who preached to the fishes. Not to be outdone, the fishes preached back to St. Andrew, as you can see in the sculpture in the garden of St. Andrew's Cathedral in downtown Honolulu.[68] It's a memorial worthy of our reason for being.

FDR

WHEN FRANKLIN DELANO ROOSEVELT was elected president of the United States, I was just starting high school. The entire nation was at the bottom of a fearsome economic depression and we were ready to pull ourselves out. FDR and his government offered us a way of decency and self-reliance, and we responded in kind. Every shop and every restaurant displayed the sign, NRA: WE DO OUR PART. "NRA" stood for "National Recovery Administration," one of a constellation of programs designed to bring the country out of the depression. FDR was our father figure. How we doted on those Fireside Chats! "My friends!"

Bon Dancing

BON DANCING is very popular in Hawai'i. It is a seasonal Buddhist celebration of the dead, who come back and dance with the living. People of all ages and denominations take part. The catchy music wafts over the various communities in turn. Bon dancing is rooted in Japan, but it has dwindled to thin kindergartner participation there. This is the "Appalachia effect"—folk culture that has died out at home flourishes in the diaspora. *Yoi yoi yoi o-sato!*

"Moose, Indian"

IT IS SAID that Oscar Wilde's last words were, "Either that wallpaper goes, or I do." Witty to the very end. People die in very different conditions and say very different things. I had a friend who died saying, "I have to get up and brush my teeth." Thoreau's last words were "Moose, Indian." Scholars conjecture about these words, but I think we should let the poor guy die in peace. He was delirious in the last stage of tuberculosis.

Dinosaur Mountain

PĀLOLO VALLEY, where our Zen center is located, is divided by a ridge at the upper end, with a little valley on each side—Waiʻomaʻo on one and Laʻi on the other. The ridge was called *Kaʻauhelemoa* by Hawaiians, after a fabulous goblin cock that was buried there. The Laʻi farmers call the ridge Dinosaur Mountain. There it stands as I look out of my window, early in the morning, burgeoning green with native and exotic trees. It is my first thrill of the day.

Old Age

Mae West said, "Old age ain't no place for sissies." Yes, that's true. One must cope with a range of afflictions, from incontinence to macular degeneration, not to mention peripheral neuropathy, strokes, and cancer—and memory loss! Yet I don't mourn my lost youth. What a confused mess I was! What time I wasted! All in all, I am really quite comfortable in these last years. Pass the marmalade!

Here I Come!

AFTER ALMOST four years of internment in Kobe, at the end of the war we civilians were on our way north by train in the first step of our repatriation. As we pulled into Yokohama station, an American military band in formal dress uniform on the platform struck up "California Here I Come!" Wow! The truth we secretly felt might somehow not be true became a joyous reality! It was happening!

Colonel Boogie March

DURING OUR INTERNMENT a couple of us were on our way back to the camp with our guard after medical appointments. A single file of perhaps ten British POWs appeared out of the dusk from a cross street. They marched in impeccable order as they whistled the "Colonel Boogie March." Even their Japanese guard, bringing up the rear, with his rifle on his shoulder, was marching and whistling with his charges. They looked straight ahead and pretended not to notice us. Many years later I saw the film *Bridge on the River Kwai*, in which the British POWs whistled the "Colonel Boogie March" as they marched to work. I went to see that movie over and over.

"Dasa Side"

THE DIALECT of Hawai'i is a kind of baby talk for adults, and its use brings forth a sense of intimacy. Carpenters and other people on the job will use the expressions "dasa side" or "dada side," rather than "the other side." They know the orthodox English perfectly well, but they enjoy sharing the diminutive, and smile at each other. The dialect is the despair of some English teachers, and a pretext that bigoted people will use to justify their prejudices, but actually it builds and maintains community. Eh, Brah!

A Cue

THE HAWAIIAN DIALECT tends to exclude people who are new to the islands, and also to exclude old-timers who lack a sense of its usage. Such people must stick to conventional English; otherwise they will seem to be talking down to their friends. They will be answered in standard language—that is their cue.

"TA DAH!"

ANOTHER PEARL from the Hawaiian dialect is "No make tada." "No make" means "Don't do." To explicate "tada," call out "TAH DAH!"—and raise the hands in triumph. "No make tada" was the modest motto of the baseball team from the community of Ewa Beach when they won the Little League Championship of the World.

Miles Carey

MILES CAREY was the principal of McKinley High School before World War II. One of his students was Miles Fukunaga, who was involved in a notorious rape case. There was another student named Fukunaga at McKinley, who was unrelated. He was razzed unmercifully about his name. The principal called an assembly and told the students to knock off their razzing, saying in defense of the student they were persecuting, "He can't help being named Fukunaga any more than I can help being named Miles." After that and to this day, Miles is a popular name for babies born in our community.

Picture Brides

MANY JAPANESE AMERICANS have a "picture bride" or two in their ancestry. Three generations or so ago, plantation workers would save enough over a period of many years to arrange for brides to join them. They sent photographs of themselves to a marriage agency in Japan, and were chosen by adventurous young women. The brides would arrive, only to find that the photos had been taken some twenty or twenty-five years earlier. They had no way to return to Japan, so they made the best of a bad bargain and settled into plantation living. Some of the marriages were really quite happy. As my Nana, Florence Page Baker, used to say, "Propinquity propinks."

Old Asian Women

ONE OF MY DOCTORS is quite elderly. He has practiced in Hawai'i for his entire professional career. I asked him, "Have you had patients who were unique to Hawai'i?" He said, "Yes. I think of old Asian women. They spent their working lives as plantation laborers. Now they are bent and skinny, but healthy and chipper. They attend the funerals of their children and sometimes their grand-children, and they live on and on."

The Turnover

AFTER THE WAR ended in August 1945, we civilian internees waited in our camp to be repatriated. The police of Kobe called our elected leaders to headquarters for a consultation. They said, "We want to build dance halls for the occupation forces. Should we have a facility for officers and another for enlisted men, or would just one facility be enough?" Western social dancing had been forbidden in Japan since 1938. The police were manifesting a national turnover that seems incredible yet was completely genuine. The emperor had spoken, and the virtue of necessity arose from the deepest place of Japanese consciousness and played itself out to the smallest detail.

The Notch

KOREAN POTTERS FLED to Japan in the sixth century when their politics got them into trouble at home. Though there was already a tradition of pottery in Japan, the native potters readily acknowledged the brilliant accomplishments of the immigrant artists. The Koreans notched the bottoms of the pots which they considered to be seconds, and they passed these on to their Japanese apprentices. The Japanese potters were so impressed by the beauty of these gifts that they notched the bottoms of their own best pots, a practice that is followed to this day.

The Green Flash

My GRANDFATHER took his turn with his fellow astronomers at Lick Observatory to host the public on Saturday evenings, when the two main telescopes were available for viewing particular stars or planets. Some people would drive up early from San Jose to watch from the parapet of the Observatory as the sun set over the coastal range beyond Santa Clara Valley. Grandfather was an imposing figure, well over six feet tall. He would stride among the early visitors and announce that soon they would see the green flash one sometimes sees just as the sun is disappearing. "The best way to see it," he proclaimed in mock seriousness, "is to turn your back on the sunset and bend over and watch for the flash there between your legs." It was an endearing sight to see the visitors lined up along the parapet, giggling at themselves, bending over to see the flash.

Finger Bowls

MY GRANDMOTHER, Jessie Thomas Aitken, affected a high style of meals, with engraved silver, crystal ware, and even finger bowls. These were small brass bowls, partly filled with water, served on a lace doily on a little plate, just before dessert. You dipped the tips of your fingers in the water, wiped them on your napkin, and then slipped the bowl with its doily beside the plate, which would then receive your helping of dessert. Once a guest from India picked up his bowl delicately with both hands and took a drink of the water. I was twelve at the time, and you can imagine my sniff of lofty superiority.

The Gurgling Magpie

THE GURGLING MAGPIE is one of many Australian songbirds distinctive to place. Its song is often inserted into the soundtrack of Australian movies. That beautiful voice is like shot silk and seems to come from underwater. Somehow it reminds me of Reginald Kell's clarinet solos in Brahms' Double Concerto.

Secret Sorrow

FOLK EXPRESSIONS can offer windows on the harshness of certain cultural norms. I first heard the expression "secret sorrow" from my Nana. It was a phrase loaded with the tragedy of love that cannot be requited. You don't hear the expression now, and its absence has its own harsh reality.

The Friendly Animals

THE RELATIONSHIP of other animals to human beings has intrigued me since my young days. The 'Elepaio would follow me along from bush to bush, chirping conversationally as I hiked the Mānoa Cliff Trail. In my middle life, a mother deer would come by and show off her baby as I sat motionless in the woods at San Juan Ridge. Then in June of 1994, I noticed the strange behavior of a thrush in a little tree just outside our front door at Pālolo. It hopped around and chirped and chirped—urgently, it seemed to me—until I got very close. I was puzzled, and mentioned its hopping and urgent chirping to my wife Anne. She didn't know what to make of its behavior either, but two days later she was dead of a brain stem stroke. I was struck by sorrow, and with awe as I recalled my prescient little friend.

"Tongues in Trees"

ROMAN CATHOLIC CLERICS have a game of opening a religious text and pointing to a passage at random, then challenging a colleague to deliver a homily on the passage. I am reminded of *As You Like It* where the Duke Senior finds "tongues in trees, books in running brooks, sermons in stones, and good in everything."[69]

The *Mejiro*

YAMADA RŌSHI and I were having tea on the lanai of Koko An when we noticed a little bird flitting around the Climbing Fig on the pillars. He asked, "What bird is that?" I responded, "It's a *mejiro* (white-eye)." The *mejiro* was introduced from Japan into Hawai'i in the 1920s, and became well settled. "*Mejiro!*" he exclaimed doubtfully. He was silent a moment as he watched the little bird. "*Chotto chigau* (A bit different)," he finally remarked.

Cinque Ports

IN THE SEVENTEENTH and eighteenth centuries, the "cinque ports" centering on the town of Rye in southeastern England were notorious for the overt smuggling practiced by city fathers. Shipments of wool and liquor were transported under guard from their docks, north to London markets. The system flourished for more than a century, and ultimately failed. The motive, however, was and still is most certainly found within and beyond the shores of England, and is hardly diverted— at least not yet.

Stephen Crane

I AM GRATEFUL to my professor of American literature, Carl Stroven, for introducing me to Stephen Crane, author of *The Red Badge of Courage*, a pacifist novel of the Civil War. The "Red Badge" is the blood of battle wounds, and Crane's writings are marked by his judicious use of colors that are completely integrated into his descriptions. His work is also marked by objective yet sympathetic presentations of the daily tribulations of the lowly, as in *Maggie: A Girl of the Streets*. The young writer can study Crane for his naturally expressed yet vivid humanism.

A Turning Point

CLAUDE ALBON STIEHL was a prominent architect in Honolulu in the years preceding World War II. He hosted a group of us young would-be writers at his home in Woodlawn. One day he had a friend sit in and listen to our efforts. This friend remarked that my poetry reminded him of Japanese and Chinese verse. I repaired to the library at once and found Asataro Miyamori's *Haiku: Ancient and Modern* and Arthur Waley's *Translations from the Chinese*. With this a train of karma got fired up, and it's still tooting along.

Sharing the Silence

ALBERT MANSON was a "bamboo," as military men in our internment camp who had retired on Guam were called. He was British by birth and perhaps the oldest man in the group, a veteran of the Boer War. He had gone completely blind, and I used to read to him. One evening as the dusk settled in and it got too dark to read, we sat together in silence. Finally he called out, "Bob!" and when I responded, he asked, "Did you ever fuck a Hottentot?" I confessed I had not, and we sat in silence once more. Then he spoke again, "You just lift that little apron, and there you are!" We had shared the silence quite differently, after all.

Uncle Max

UNCLE MAX was a veteran of World War I who suffered from what we now call post-traumatic stress disorder. He belted out the Marine Hymn in his fine baritone voice, over and over, accompanying himself on the family player-piano. Fortunately he was rescued by Margaret, a Quaker girl. They married and raised two children. They conversed in the Quaker mode—"Can thee do the shopping today?" They lived out their lives in a California town, he as a school teacher and she as a postal clerk. Margaret was just being herself, but what a self she was!

The Foreign Groom

ONE OF MANY intriguing exhibits at the Honolulu Academy of Arts is a set of little Tang period polo players, three women and their foreign groom, possibly Iranian. With his beard and homely alien face he stands forth as himself, and for us he stands for the mix of nationalities possible in those early days. The Tang period ran from the seventh century through the early tenth—Marco Polo did not visit China for another four centuries. There is the groom, focused on whacking the ball for all time.

Holocaust Survivors

A FRIEND OF MINE and her twin sister are daughters of Holocaust survivors. Their mother died soon after World War II, and they were raised by their father. Once when the girls were still small, he took them to northern Italy to see the old family home. They found it, and the new owner admitted them before the father had introduced himself completely. There in the living room was his beloved piano—there was his furniture—there were his pictures and books. The new owner soon realized the identity of his guests, and became hostile and asked them to leave. The father was profoundly upset, and when they drove away he was completely reckless on the mountain roads. The little girls were terrified. Finally the car actually went over the edge, but it stuck on a shelf above a steep canyon. The father came to his senses at last, but not before his daughters had also experienced some of their father's horror.

Counting Seconds

WHEN I WAS a boy, my grandmother taught me how to count seconds, the intervals of time: "One blue tomcat, two blue tomcat, three blue tomcat," and so on. I think of her now as I do my geriatric exercises, some eighty years later. Thank you Grandmother, thank you Grandmother, thank you Grandmother . . .

Pleasant Memories

NELSON FOSTER WHEELED me around the Hawai'i State Art Museum and there we saw a beautiful little painting by Sunao Hironaka, whom I knew when I was thirteen. His wife Grace attended the University of Hawai'i and worked for us part-time, helping my mother around the house and looking after us boys. She was the light of our young lives and the pet of our parents. What a rush of pleasant memories that little painting evoked!

Grandmother's Admonitions

WHEN I WAS TWELVE, my grandmother wrote in my Memory Book, "Grandmother says, 'Cultivate a sense of proportion, and don't dramatize your emotions.'" A lifetime later, students at the Maui Zendo found the little book in one of my boxes, and with glee read Grandmother's admonitions aloud to the group. What a razzing I took!

Humane Antennae

THE MONK UNZAN PFENNIG was my caregiver when I lived on the Big Island. Once a month he flies here to Oʻahu to spell my regular caregivers for a weekend. Once we visited the Waikiki Aquarium and had lunch nearby. We had a bit of shopping to do, so we planned to stop at an ABC store on our way home, but there was no parking anywhere. Finally we slipped into a no-parking zone next to a big hotel. Unzan went off and left me waiting in the car. A security person appeared and asked me, "May I help you?" "Yes," I said. "Bring me a chocolate mint." He looked at me closely—I was ninety years old, you know. He said, "Okay." He went off and did not come back. Unzan returned with his purchases and we drove home. I liked that security person. He was someone with his humane antennae fully extended.

Reading the Book

ONE OF MY school mates at the University of Hawai'i was Norman Chung, scion of a prominent business family. He carried a 4.0 grade-point average while serving as editor of *Ka Leo*, the weekly student newspaper. One day I asked him how he did it, and he said, "I have a simple weapon. It's called 'Reading the Book.'" Simone Weil would have loved that response.

Incredibly Naïve

DURING ONE of my early stays in Japan, a neighbor who had just graduated from high school one day announced, excited and pleased, that she had been hired as a telephone operator. "It will allow me to be of service to my community," she said. I thought she was being incredibly naïve, but I was new to Japanese attitudes.

Liquid Sunshine

It RAINS a lot in Hawai'i, particularly in Wai'oma'o, the part of Pālolo Valley where we live. There are many kinds of rain, including "liquid sunshine," as we called it as children, when it sprinkles on a bright day. The sun shines through the light rain and the effect is lovely. The Hawaiians call this phenomenon *kilihune*. They have hundreds of words for the many kinds of rain, with the exact number dependent on the linguist doing the counting.[70] In any case the total far exceeds the number of words in the Inuit language for different kinds of snow, which is variously counted at around thirty.

All Things Are under the Law
of Change

IN 1928, when I was a boy living with my grandparents at the Observatory on Mt. Hamilton, the little community was served by a "coach" consisting of an aged van driven from San Jose. The driver, Mr. Roper, would have one or two passengers, but his main task was to deliver groceries and the mail. I remember two fallen-in buildings on the way to the top, at Grand View and Smith Creek. These had served as hotels in the old days of coaches drawn by teams of horses, where the passengers would stay overnight and new teams of horses would take over. In 1928 the old structures and their stables stood empty and decrepit, and today, of course, they are gone, along with Mr. Roper and his van. The present residents all have cars, and they do their own shopping in San Jose, or even San Francisco. They probably smile at the old photographs. But nothing survives after all—nothing at all.

A Fine Memory

ONE OF MY old friends marveled that I retained a fine memory for my age. I explained that I have developed an elaborate system of mnemonics, and that I depend heavily on spell-check and search engines on my computer. I did not mention that I couldn't remember her name.

Grandpa Baker's Failure

My GRANDPA, James Bartlett Baker, was a trusted family physician. He ended up in Lake County, California, where he presided over the birth of all the babies born in a period of fifteen years. He was "Grandpa the Fixer" for me as a small child, when I brought him my busted toys. He was an intuitive diagnostician, an infallible obstetrician, and he could repair almost anything. Sadly, he married wrong and after fifty years of earnest endeavor, he couldn't make things right. He couldn't attain the measure of human happiness that we all hope for ourselves.

Impressing Mom and Dad

Patricia Diaz Dennis is a distinguished attorney living in Washington, DC. I heard her tell this story on television while I was surfing channels during a lung treatment one evening. It seems that when she was sworn in as Assistant Secretary of State for Human Rights and Humanitarian Affairs in 1992, her parents were given seats of honor at the ceremony. They were Mexican American, he a former sergeant in the U.S. army, she a civilian employee of the army with a GS-2 rating. They were of the earth, earthy, and were not easily awed. Even a prestigious ceremony for their own daughter did not impress them. They were greeted by President George H. W. Bush, and were not impressed. They were given a special tour of the White House and were shown their daughter's office. They met her staff and were still not impressed. Mrs. Diaz opened a file drawer there in her daughter's office, and noticed files labeled GS-10, GS-11, and GS-12. "Do you supervise GS-12s?" she asked. "Yes, I do," her daughter answered. "What is your secretary's rating?" "GS-8," was the reply. "My God!" Mrs. Diaz exclaimed. "My General is a GS-8!" Mom and Dad were impressed at last.

Mother's Inability

MY MOTHER, Gladys Baker Aitken, graduated from the University of California in 1912 with a major in Latin and a minor in Greek. In Honolulu, she was president of the Friends of the Library for a term, and for many years was chair of the book review section of the American Association of University Women. She raised two sons. However, she was not able to lay her mother's intrusive compulsions to rest. Her benefice and talent were no match for a relentless, negative will that seemed to demand her constant attention and energy. This karma affected her marriage, and ultimately me, I'm sure, though I lack the insight to say just how.

The Patriot

My father was jingoistic—no two ways about it. When we boys were young, the family would go for a drive on Sunday afternoons. If we passed a service station that was flying the Stars and Stripes after sunset, he would stop the car and tell the proprietor to take it down. Old Glory is not supposed to fly after dark. We boys would slide down in our seats in embarrassment. He failed the physical for entry into the army for World War I, and was deeply disappointed. As time went on, he studied for the tests to become an officer, and just before World War II he passed his physical and was commissioned a second lieutenant (at the age of fifty). He served with distinction in the China-Burma-India Theater and came home a major. He had done his duty at last.

Dad's Indiscretion

MY FATHER SPENT time on the island of Tubuai in French Polynesia doing ethnological research from 1920 to 1922, as part of the Bayard Dominick Expedition of the Bishop Museum. He became very ill and during his convalescence, apparently just once, he slipped into bed with his caregiver. More than half a century later, after he had lived out his life, my brother found a letter in Dad's papers that indicated we had a half-sister, Tehina Tenuri. We were delighted. To shorten a very long story, Malcolm and his wife Pat, Anne and I—and later Tom and other Aitkens—traveled to Tubuai and then Tahiti, and visited Tehina and her nine children and their innumerable children and *their* innumerable children and innumerable, innumerable cousins and other connections. Many of them have visited us, and one of the youngest of Tehina's granddaughters is at this writing attending the University of Hawai'i. One indiscretion—and wow!

Trick or Treat

"TRICK OR TREAT," chant the piping voices as the little charmers in their creative costumes hold out baggies for candy. They have no idea what their chant implies. Not too long ago the children were put to bed early while their nasty big brothers tricked the neighborhood with overturned garbage cans and obscene messages painted on the minister's garage. "Trick or treat" actually has origins in ancient Europe, passing to medieval times, where in England, for example, good-hearted celebrators dressed as ghouls or ghosts went "a-souling" door to door on All Souls' Eve to beg food for the poor. In the 1930s, parents in Montana and Illinois spontaneously reverted to the original tradition of giving, when they couldn't bear the messy garbage on their front lawns. It is once again a holiday that revives the human spirit, and our tiny revelers today unknowingly evoke their hidden underpinnings.

The Human Spirit

THE FABLES OF Robert Louis Stevenson inform his novels. His story "The Touchstone" informs my very life.[71] His oeuvre has not, unfortunately, stood the critical test of time unscathed. Leo Tolstoy, the creative hero who wrote *War and Peace*, *Anna Karenina*, and other monumental novels, also wrote the fable "How Much Land Does a Man Need?"—first called "Does a Man Need Much Land?"[72] Chekhov called it the best short story ever written. Stevenson and Tolstoy lived in almost the same era and RLS couldn't help but know that he had an elder brother he had never met. There is always a bigger flea.

Expelled

I ATTENDED first grade at Central Grammar School in Honolulu. In those days children were not promoted from grade to grade if their work was unsatisfactory. There were rowdy eight-year-olds who sat in the back of the classroom with a recalcitrant eleven-year-old among them named Matthew. He was a troublemaker, and one day during recess he pushed a little girl off the slide and she broke her arm. A lady from the superintendent's office came to investigate. She called Matthew before the class and held up a large card that contained a simple sentence. "Read that for us," she said. He couldn't read the first word. The next day he didn't come to school and we never saw him again. I think of him sometimes, and wonder what became of him.

The Master

THAT MASTER of the miniature, Henry David Thoreau, spent a pleasant Sunday afternoon in May rowing on the river with his sister. They heard the faint mewing of a kitten, so they pulled over to the bank, and as he wrote later in his journal:

> Leaving its mewing, it came scrambling over the stones as fast as its weak legs would permit straight to me. I took it up and dropped it into the boat, but while I was pushing off it ran to Sophia, who held it while we rowed homeward. Evidently it had not been weaned—was smaller than we remembered that kittens ever were—almost infinitely small; yet it had hailed a boat, its life being in danger, and saved itself. Its performance, considering its age and amount of experience, was more wonderful than that of any young mathematician or musician that I have read of.[73]

Advertisement

WHEN I WAS a boy, I read everything I could lay my hands on, including magazine advertisements. I was puzzled by some of the ads. For example, there was one for cleaning powder that carried the slogan, "Hasn't scratched yet." *Well*, I thought, *what about in a few months? What then?* I also puzzled over an ad for a salt company. The picture showed a little girl carrying a container of salt that was pouring forth as she walked in the rain. The caption read, "When it rains, it pours." *Well*, I thought, *she's wasteful, she's careless*. I also puzzled over an ad for an automobile tire company. It showed a little girl in a nightgown, yawning, holding a tire. The caption read, "Time to retire." I thought that was the worst joke I'd ever read. In those days, nobody questioned the ad for a car company that read, "Ask the man who owns one." Today I can't read the ads.

Carrying the Dog

ON SEVERAL OCCASIONS when she was driving into town, my secretary, Carolyn Glass, noticed an elderly Japanese woman carrying a little dog along the sidewalk. Commenting on this to a friend, she said, "I suppose the little dog was old or sick." Her friend said, "Probably not; elderly Japanese women will carry a dog so its feet won't get dirty."

Owly-Growly

WHEN IT WAS available, Union soldiers in the Civil War were served Owly-Growly for breakfast. This was an omelet made with diced bread and pieces of bacon, onion, tomato, and green pepper. When we were boys, my brother and I were served Owly-Growly too, and we thought of our great-grandfather, who was still living at that time. I wonder if the tradition is still observed somewhere.

Saimin

SAIMIN IS a popular noodle dish in Hawai'i, and is sold by the plastic cup in markets. An eight-year-old member of a family I know demands it for his breakfast, lunch, and dinner. His parents accede without a murmur. After all, he will not be eight years old for long, and his addiction can hardly last. If his compulsion was repressed and he was forced to eat balanced meals, would that repression survive in other ways? It might.

Unexpurgated Mother Goose

I KNEW THAT *Grimm's Fairy Tales* had been expurgated, but I didn't know about Mother Goose until my granddaughter Gina appeared and her dad found the original for her:

> Bah, bah, black sheep,
> Have you any wool?
> Yes, marry, have I,
> Three bags full;
> One for my master,
> One for my dame,
> But none for the little boy
> Who cries in the lane.[74]

This is an influence that will help my granddaughter grow up to be a woman who is in touch with herself, enabled to face the acquisitive system without illusion.

Dr. Maher

My neurologist is Leo M. Maher, MD. (I use his name with his permission.) He is Chinese American, and I thought for a long time that he had been adopted as a child. It turns out, however, that he is really "Maher" and his distant ancestor was a Dutch merchant who settled in Canton or some other seaport town. He married and founded a dynasty. Dr. Maher's grandfather migrated to the United States and Mah-erh became Maher again. In keeping with his legacy, Dr. Maher is unconventional in his views and we talk social justice as much as we talk neuropathy. He's a true friend.

The Puffer Fish

THE PUFFER FISH is in the Tetraodontidae family and flourishes in estuary waters. Though it contains enough poison to kill thirty people, it is delicious if it is skillfully prepared—so it is said. A popular Japanese proverb sums up the situation: "To those who have never tasted the puffer fish, we cannot speak of its flavor."[75] It takes trust in the cook, of course.

Seahorses

SEAHORSES JUST FLOAT around and don't seem to do much, but they are really fascinating creatures. When they mate, the female expels her egg and the male puts it into a pouch in his tummy and becomes pregnant. He gives birth to the baby seahorse and nurtures it for its brief spell to adulthood. You might not expect such tiny creatures to bond with each other, but male and female seahorses establish a lifetime relationship. In Australian waters, the Leafy Sea Dragon is related to the seahorse, but looks exactly like a piece of seaweed. It floats around just like its cousins elsewhere.

The Music of the Spheres

SOMEONE TOLD ME about hearing the music of the spheres one starry night. He had never heard it before, and didn't know that others had heard it too, down through the millennia. A bit later, in broad daylight, he heard the same heavenly sounds on a city street. It was an extraordinary revelation to find they came from a music store playing a Bach organ prelude! When I heard this story, I thought of myself as a twelve-year-old boy peering through the thirty-six-inch refractor at Lick Observatory. I heard the same glorious music as I brought the Pleiades, Saturn, or Jupiter into my view, floating out there. What a gift! And how blessed was Johann Sebastian Bach! How blessed we are to hear him! Over and over I listen to Christopher Herrick playing Bach's Organ Miniatures.[76] Ah, that celestial music, so vital to Dante's experience! It is the sound of contrapuntal attraction that gives life to the universe and holds it together. It confirms human beings and their society at last. Hear the being of humanity—of animals, stones, clouds, and vast nebulae! The awesome Net of Indra stands forth clearly.

Notes

1 Mu (Japanese). No; does not have. The first case of Zen Buddhist practice, from Case 1 of the *Wumenguan*. "A monk asked Zhaozhou in all earnestness, 'Has the dog Buddha-nature or not?' Zhaozhou said, 'Mu.'" Zenkei Shibayama, *The Gateless Barrier: Zen Comments on the Mumonkan* (Boston: Shambhala, 2000), p. 19.

2 Bodhisattva (Sanskrit). One on the path to realization; one who is realized; one who makes it possible for others to be realized; a figure in the Buddhist pantheon.

3 Kanzeon or Kannon (Japanese), Guanyin (Chinese). The one who harkens to the sounds of the world—the Incarnation of Compassion.

4 Yamada Kōun Rōshi (1907-1989). Japanese master of the Sanbō Kyōdan school; teacher of Westerners. Teacher of Robert Aitken.

5 Dōjō (Japanese). The training hall or zendo. One's own place of realization.

6 Yamamoto Gempō Rōshi (1866-1961). Japanese Rinzai master of Ryūtakuji Monastery; teacher of Nakagawa Sōen.

7 Teishō (Japanese). The Dharma presented by the Rōshi in a public talk.

8 Dharma (Sanskrit). Religious, secular, or natural law; the Law of Karma; Buddha Dharma or Tao; teaching; the Dharmakāya. With a lowercase "d," a phenomenon or thing.

9 Zazen (Japanese). Seated Zen Buddhist practice.

10 Nyogen Senzaki Sensei (1876-1958). First Japanese Zen teacher to settle in the West; a disciple of Shaku Sōen Zenji.

11 Shaku Sōen Zenji (1859-1919). Japanese master of Engaku Monastery in Kitakamakura. He introduced Zen to the West at the World Parliament of Religions in Chicago in 1892.

12 Eightfold Path. The ideals and practice of Right Views, Right Thoughts, Right Speech, Right Conduct, Right Livelihood, Right Effort or Lifestyle, Right Recollection, and Right Absorption (in keeping with the insubstantial nature of the Self, Mutual Interdependence, and the sacred nature of each Being). The way of freeing oneself from Duhkha.

13 Hisao Inagaki with P. G. O'Neill, *A Dictionary of Japanese Buddhist Terms* (Kyoto: Nagata Bunshodo, 1984), p. 93.

14 Burtin Watson, trans., *The Vimalakirti Sutra*, (New York: Columbia University Press, 1997).

15 Kōan (Japanese). Universal/particular. A presentation of the harmony of the universal and the particular. A theme of zazen to be made clear. A classic Zen story.

16 Seikan Hasegawa, *The Cave of Poison Grass: Essays on the Hannya Sutra* (Arlington, VA: Great Ocean Publishers, 1975), p. 12; fn. 6; p. 169.

17 Robert Aitken, *Encouraging Words: Zen Buddhist Teachings for Western Students* (New York and San Francisco: Pantheon Books, 1993), p. 173.

18 Nakagawa Sōen Rōshi (1907-1984). Japanese Zen master of Ryūtakuji Monastery; teacher of Westerners. A haiku poet.

19 D. T. Suzuki, *Manual of Zen Buddhism* (New York: Grove Press, 1960), pp. 135-144.

20 Watson, *The Vimalakirti Sutra*, p. 44.

21 Ino (Japanese). The leader of chanting the sutras.

22 Jukai (Japanese). The ceremony of accepting the Buddha as one's teacher and the Precepts as guides.

23 Rakusu (Japanese). The priest's robe, cut short for lay students, presented to initiates as part of the Jukai ceremony.

24 Arthur Braverman, trans., *Mud and Water: The Collected Teachings of Zen Master Bassui* (Boston: Wisdom Publications, 2002), p. 187.

25 Aitken, *Encouraging Words*, p. 178.

26 Nyogen Senzaki and Ruth Stout McCandless, *Buddhism and Zen* (New York: Philosophical Library, 1953), p. 84.

27 Zhaozhou Congshen (778-897). An important Chinese master from whom we have the kōan "Mu." See Note 1.

28 Oshō. The priest—in this case, soon-to-be Rōshi.

29 See Note 3.

30 Mudrā (Sanskrit). A seal or sign; hand or finger position or gesture that presents an aspect of the Dharma.

31 "Song of Zazen." Aitken, *Encouraging Words*, pp. 179-180. Hakuin Ekaku Zenji (1685-1768). Japanese Rinzai master, ancestor of all contemporary Rinzai teachers.

32 Dokusan (Japanese). "To work alone"; personal interview with the Rōshi during formal practice.

33 Dale S. Wright, *Philosophical Meditations on Zen Buddhism* (Cambridge Unversity, 1998), p. 74.

34 Sesshin (Japanese). To touch, receive, and convey the Mind; the intensive Zen retreat of three to seven days.

35 Zendo (Japanese). Zen hall; Zen center. Dōjō.

36 Donald Keene, trans., *Essays in Idleness: The Tsurezuregusa of Kenkō* (NewYork: Columbia University Press, 1967), p. 40.

37 Watson, *The Vimalakirti Sutra*, p. 25.

38 Yasutani Haku'un Rōshi (1895-1973). Japanese founder of the Sanbō Kyōdan; teacher of Yamada Kōun and of Westerners.

39 Bodhidharma (sixth century). Legendary Indian or West Asian founder of Chan Buddhism; archetype for steadfast practice.

40 Suzuki Shunryū Rōshi (1904-1971). Japanese Sōtō teacher; founder and first abbot of the Zen Center of San Francisco.

41 Maezumi Taizan Rōshi (1931-1995). A Japanese Zen teacher who founded the Zen Center of Los Angeles and influenced the growth of Zen in the West. Successor of Hakujun Kuroda Rōshi, Ōsaka Kōryū Rōshi, and Yasutani Haku'un Rōshi.

42 Watson, *The Vimalakirti Sutra*, pp. 90-92.

43 Holly Stevens, ed., *Wallace Stevens: The Palm at the End of the Mind* (New York: Vintage Books, 1971), p. 54.

44 Sasaki Shigetsu Rōshi, also known as Sokei An (1882-1945). The first Zen master to settle in the United States, founder of the First Zen Institute of America, husband of Ruth Fuller Sasaki.

45 Sonja Arntzen, *Ikkyū and the Crazy Cloud Anthology* (Tokyo: University of Tokyo Press, 1986), p. 158.

46 Danxia Tianran (739-824). D. T. Suzuki, *Sengai: The Zen of Ink and Paper* (Boston and London: Shambhala, 1999), pp. 86-87.

47 Hong Zicheng (1593-1665). A Chinese philosopher who lived during the end of the Ming dynasty and wrote the *Caigentan*,

translated as *Vegetable Roots Discourse: Wisdom from Ming China on Life and Living*, by Robert Aitken with Daniel Kwok (Berkeley, CA: Counterpoint, 2006), p. 54.

48 Kinhin (Japanese). "Walking verification," sutra walk; the formal walk between periods of zazen.

49 Ikkyū Sōjun Zenji (1374-1481). Arntzen, *Ikkyū and the Crazy Cloud Anthology*, p. 150.

50 D. T. Suzuki (1870-1966). Japanese lay disciple of Shaku Sōen; the scholar most responsible for introducing Zen to the West.

51 Satori (Japanese). Enlightenment; the condition ofr (sometimes) the experience of realization.

52 Kenshō (Japanese). True nature, realization.

53 Zenkei Shibayama Rōshi (1894-1974). Abbot of the Rinzai monastery Nanzenji in Kyoto. Author of *The Gateless Barrier*.

54 Dōgen Kigen (1200-1253). Venerated as the Japanese founder of the Sōtō tradition.

55 Dungshan Liangjie (807-869). Dharma heir of Yunyan Tansheng. Founder of the Caodong (Sōtō) school. Gave transmission to Yunju Daoying.

56 Shibayama, *The Gateless Barrier*, p. 19.

57 Precepts. In Mahayana, the Sixteen Bodhisattva Precepts are: the Three Vows of Refuge in the Three Treasures; the Three Pure Precepts of avoiding evil, practicing good, and saving the many beings; and the Ten Grave Precepts of not killing, not stealing, not misusing sex, not speaking falsely, not giving or taking drugs, not discussing faults of others, not praising oneself while abusing others, not sparing the Dharma assets, not indulging in anger, and not defaming the Three Treasures.

58 Aitken, *Encouraging Words,* p. 179. Hakuin Ekaku (1686-1769), Japanese Rinzai Zen master, from whom all contemporary Rinzai masters are descended.

59 Thomas Traherne, *Centuries of Meditation* (London: Christian Classics Ethereal Library manuscript) I: 29-30.

60 Albert Camus, *The Myth of Sisyphus and Other Essays* (New York: Vintage Books, 1955).

61 Hyder Edward Rollins, ed., *The Letters of John Keats, 1814-1821,* Vols. 1 and 2 (Cambridge, MA: Harvard University Press, 1958), p. 123.

62 Logan Pearsall Smith, *All Trivia* (New York: Harcourt Brace & Company, 1947).

63 Barbara Bernard Smith et al., eds., *The Queen's Song Book* (Honolulu: Hui Hanai, 1999).

64 Watson, *The Vimalakirti Sutra*, p. 65.

65 Kenneth Rexroth, *The Phoenix and the Tortoise* (New York: New Directions, 1944), p. 75.

66 Desmond Tutu, "Goodness Is Powerful" (New York: Democracy Now! transcript, Nov. 27, 2007).

67 Susan Griffin, *A Chorus of Stones: The Private Life of War* (New York: Anchor/Doubleday, 1992), p. 179.

68 The figure of St. Andrew is the sculpture of Ivan Mestrovic; the fishes are by Robert Laurent.

69 *As You Like It*, ii. 1.

70 Conversation with Manu Meyer, Associate Professor of Education, University of Hawai'i at Hilo, October 15, 2007.

71 Robert Louis Stevenson, *Fables* (New York: Charles Scribner's Sons, 1905), p. 61.

72 Leo Tolstoy, *How Much Land Does a Man Need? And Other Stories* (New York: Penguin Classics, 1994).

73 Odell Shephard, ed., *The Heart of Thoreau's Journals* (Boston and New York: Houghton Mifflin, 1927), p. 171.

74 Eulie Osgood Grover, ed., *Mother Goose: The Original Volland Edition* (New York: Derrydale Books, 1997).

75 R. H. Blythe. *Zen in English Literature and Oriental Classics* (Tokyo: Hokuseido Press, 1942), p. 69.

76 Christopher Herrick, *Bach: Organ Miniatures* (London: Hyperion Records, 1996).

Acknowledgments

For Editorial Support:

Jack Shoemaker, Jane Vandenburgh, Carolyn Glass,
Nelson Foster, Roxanna Aliaga, Laura Mazer, Trish
Hoard, Anne Connolly, Greg Shepherd, Joe Rothstein,
Tom Aitken, Michael Kieran, Gillian Coote, David
Derauf, Manu Meyer, Victoria Austin, Jerry Ono,
Unzan T. H. Pfennig, Barry McMahon, Dorsey
Cummings, John Clark, Yuko Ishimura, Lo Maher,
and Keiki Hatano.

For Personal Support:

Carolyn Glass, Tom Aitken, Michael Kieran, Supiesi
"Supi" Lauaki, Miliame "Mili" Kaihau, Lilieta "Lil"
'Unga, Ginger Ikenberry, Joe Rothstein, and members
of the Honolulu Diamond Sangha.

Printed in the United States
by Baker & Taylor Publisher Services